MASTERING THE NLP COMMUNICATION MODEL

Tim Brunson, PhD

The International Hypnosis Research Institute, LLC

CONTENTS

INTRODUCTION

Neuro-Linguistic Programming, or NLP, is a set of theories related to human communication, learning, and behavior that is associated with a collection of rather simple techniques. It has been used successfully in psychotherapy, life coaching, management consulting, learning, and even health care. Although it was originally promoted as a form of rapid psychotherapy, due to the simplistic nature of the techniques, it was quickly adopted by many self-help promoters.

Unlike many forms of psychotherapy, NLP rapidly gained popularity and was adopted by many practitioners without the normal more cautious approaches that traditionally came out of universities with their countless literature using accepted, peer-reviewed studies. This and the fact that practitioners were claiming results in a fraction of the time compared to traditional psychoanalysis and other psychotherapy led to wide suspicion and condemnation by many organizations around the globe.

As will be mentioned in a moment, NLP has a strong relationship with Ericksonian hypnotherapy. Therefore, many hypnotherapists such as me started off their interest in human transformation by becoming certified in NLP.

NLP training often leads to formal practitioner or master practitioner certifications, each requiring over 130 hours of formal classroom instruction. Some go on to achieve a trainer's certification, which typically lasts three weeks with the last week consisting of a comprehensive written exam and supervised practical demonstrations. Due to the amount of dedication required to complete formal training, several schools have developed truncated intensives that attempt to compact a certain level of training into ten or fewer days. Generally, this does not allow the student enough time to integrate the information between classes. As much of NLP training involves the observation of human behavior, the more lengthy, non-compressed approach more than likely will produce a superior practitioner.

THE ORIGINS OF NLP

NLP originated predominantly from the work of Richard Bandler, who was a student at the University of California, Santa Cruz, and John Grinder, one of his lecturers. The very first influences came from the late Gestalt therapist Fritz Perls and family therapist Virginia Satir. Later they drew additional ideas from the work of Gregory Bateson and Alfred Korzybski, particularly when it came to modeling human behavior and ideas. One of the most important contributions came from an exhaustive study of the work of Milton H. Erickson, MD. It was Erickson's work that led them to recognize the value of what they called the Milton model, which they described as being vague and metaphoric. The other predominant models developed by Bandler, Grinder, and their initial students included anchoring, reframing, submodalities, perceptual positions, and representational systems.

WHY STUDY NLP?

The two words that you constantly hear during NLP training are modeling and techniques. Much of the field focuses on the ability to summarize human behavior into workable models and then develop techniques based upon them in order to create a desired change.

Models can be looked at both as general theoretical constructs that help a person understand a class of behavior and as a simplification of a specific behavior such as expressing a fear or phobia, or the techniques used by an expert golfer or speller. By understanding a general model, such as the NLP Communications Model, which I will discuss next, a clinician can quickly detect faulty expressions and move a subject toward better clarity and understanding. And, if a coach or trainer fully understands the true nature of expert performance of one person, then just maybe they can install the same quality behavior in another.

Hopefully, this brief explanation concerning the utility of NLP models and techniques will help you better understand the value of learning this field. As a clinician I recognize the opportunities that arise when I better grasp a subject's mental function and find myself using a specific methodology for an effective intervention. As a trainer or coach, I can increase my abilities to understand ideal performance and help a client replicate and model it. Essentially, this is where the value of NLP resides.

The widespread acceptance of NLP, which happened almost simultaneously with the human potential movement, came from observable results. As I said earlier, as these results originated with a wide range of practitioners, many of whom who had absolutely no credentials in psychology or psychiatry, and not within academic or scientific institutions, many institutional stake-holders rejected NLP and continue to avoid it as part of mainstream clinical education. However, there has almost always been a significant clinical interest in NLP as a form of rapid therapy.

THE NLP COMMUNICATIONS MODEL

The one model that I feel is at the heart of Neuro-Linguistic Programming is the NLP Communications Model. Essentially, it attempts to explain the process that begins with external events and ends in specific and discreet human behavior.

A major contribution was the realization that we filter our perceptions. Yes, we delete certain aspects of what we perceive. As our brain naturally and quickly attempts to understand perceptual input, we tend to generalize by categorizing external objects by what they are like or unlike. And, then we often distort our perceptions as we try to fit them into our preconceived or pre-programmed patterns.

This filtering can happen either consciously or below conscious awareness. This results in the formation of an internal representation – which is the byprod-uct of our desire to understand. This creates an internal state such as awe, fear, happiness, comfort, etc. In turn, this is expressed by our physiology. The physiological manifestation of a state may be as obvious as a change in posture or expression. It may also be as subtle as an alteration of galvanic skin response (GSR), periph-eral skin temperature, or any other biofeedback-like re-sponse.

While the model claims that it is state that generates behavior, this was not fully explained until later when Bandler began discussing a person's drive to preserve the known and familiar.

UNDERSTANDING DELETIONS, GENERALIZATIONS, AND DISTORTIONS

When attempting to understand how a person filters input, noticing their meta-programs, values, beliefs, decisions, and memories will be critical.

You may have never heard of the term meta-program. First, think of a program as a strategy. Over the years people develop strategies that consist of automatic ways in which they feel comfortable reacting to their external environment.

For instance, consider what is called sorting styles. One person may sort memories by the dates of important events in their life, by what they were wearing, where they were living, or even by to whom they were married or dating. Another person may decide to explain an object or event by to what it is similar or different. Some sort by considering themselves first; others focus primarily on others. These are just a few examples of meta-programs. By the way, the word "meta" means beyond.

In the NLP context a meta-program would represent a strategy that seems to permeate a variety of contextual behaviors. The NLP meta-programs were derived from the advanced linguistic patterns developed by Erickson.

Values and beliefs are also extremely important filters. A value is a filter that expresses what a person feels is important. A belief is a psychological state in which an individual holds a proposition or premise to be true. When an external event is perceived, a person will develop an internal representation, state, and behavior based upon their value and belief filters.

For instance, if I observe an act of compassion or cruelty, my value filters will create a specific physiological state and may precipitate action on my part. On the other hand, if I see an object drop from a tall building, my belief expectations will lead me to assume that it will fall. Of course, if it floats instead, I may experience momentary discomfort until my filters readjust to accommodate the new reality.

Please realize that way too often people sloppily misuse and mix up the terms belief and thought or thinking. Again, a belief is a psychological state related to a presumed truth. Hence, I believe – not think – that the ball will fall when dropped.

Thinking and thought refer to a process in which a pattern or form is created without the reliance on perception. Thought formation – which is also known as thinking – may be affected a priori or post by belief filters. However, an educated individual should understand that the two are extremely different. Nevertheless, a clinical subject will often be observed misusing the two concepts.

The only reason that I bring this up here is to emphasize that in NLP the practitioner normally focuses on changing a subject's thought process rather than attempting to alter their beliefs. Of course, reframing a belief could also serve as a therapeutic intervention. It is important for the operator to understand which one they are seeking to alter – the process or the state. Generally, the best way to alter a dysfunctional state (or belief system) is to get the subject to change their processes by getting them to think differently. This is one of the fundamental goals of NLP.

VAKOG: CHANNELS FOR COMMUNICATION

As perception is so critical to NLP theory and practice, it is vital that students fully understand the role of perceptual modalities. There are three primary and two secondary perceptual modalities discussed in NLP. The three primary ones are visual, auditory, and kinesthetic. The two secondary ones, gustatory and olfactory, are normally considered related to the kinesthetic modality. These can be abbreviated as VAKOG.

People receive perceptual input through what they see, hear, feel, taste, and smell. Once these perceptions are filtered, they then affect a subject's internal representation, state, behavior, and physiology.

RECOGNIZING PREFERRED COMMUNICATIONS STYLES

One of the first skills that a practitioner student is exposed to is how to recognize a person's preferred communication channel or modality. This is the same as saying that while all five channels are available, a person would ordinarily prefer to be communicated with one. For instance, when teaching a complex task, some people would prefer to be shown, others want a detailed explanation, and others will never learn the task until they are able to do it themselves. These people are visual, auditory, and kinesthetic learners, respectively.

You may not have picked up on one other thing that I just said. I said that almost everyone has a preferred communication channel. However, in stressful situations that may change. A visual or auditory person can quickly become kinesthetic during an emergency. Or a kinesthetic one could become more auditory. For instance, a slow talking kinesthetic person may tend to emphasize clarity of verbal expression when stressed or a visual may emotionally seize up and slow down their speech when threatened.

I was also taught initially that people who have a specific modality preference may choose their occupation accordingly. A hard charging business executive may be a visual, a radio announcer or schoolteacher an auditory, and a florist, chef, or massage therapist a kinesthetic.

You can also pick up preferred modalities by noticing the frequency of various predicates. The use of words like see, demonstrate, and show would indicate a visual person, explain, tell, relate, an auditory, and feel and sense, a kinesthetic. Also, you will run into people who often say that something just stinks or smells. They are olfactory learners. Or, if the say that something leaves a bad taste in their mouths, they are gustatory learners.

Also notice the way people stand – including posture – gesture and speak. A visual typically will speak faster and use their hands to gesture at the chest or higher level. An auditory will speak more deliberately and gesture more at the waist to chest level. Then the kinesthetic will speak relatively slower as they always insist at staying in touch with their feelings and gesture from the waist level down.

Why is this important? In *Developing Instant Rapport*, which is the next book in this series, I will discuss the importance of achieving rapport and the value of pacing and leading another person. Understanding their preferred style is critical to your efforts in these areas. What NLP trainers say is that you want to meet your subject within their model of the world. If their world is a kinesthetic one and you are a visual, then you are already at a disadvantage. However, if you can learn to meet them in their model and truly speak their language you can then lead them to a more functional state or to install excellence.

What I just began discussing is your need for flexibility. One of the most profound rules of NLP is the Law of Requisite Variety. Essentially, this states that "The element of the system that possess the most flexibility will serve as a catalyst for that system." If you as a clinician, coach, or trainer want to be a transformative catalyst with another person, you must show behavioral flexibility. When considering preferred communication modalities, your ability to alter your expressions – which is perceived by your subject – to match with how they prefer to be communicated, then you will find that you connect more rapidly. However, that is not to say that there will not be times that you wish to alter your style. Once you have connected, sometimes it will be necessary for you to be flexible in order to begin the change process in your subject. This will be discussed further as this book and series progresses.

STATE AND BEHAVIOR

As I conclude, I want to once again return to the state/behavior linkage that is so important to NLP theory. The goal is almost always to change a person's state. Remember also that it is the state, which I often call a limbic phenomenon, that is intimately linked to the belief and values filter. When a dysfunction or lack of self-actualization exists, then it is time for a state change. Indeed, this is a fundamental NLP concept. The question is how this occurs.

The NLP Communication Model focuses on how the process typically occurs. It shows how perceptions eventually result in reactive behavior. On the other hand, change frequently happens by getting the subject to move in reverse on the model. What I mean here is that almost all NLP interventions work by getting the subject to change their behavior, which in turn alters their physiology, their state, their internal representations, and eventually challenges their filters – which are probably the root of most of their problems in the first place.

Again, therefore I insist on clarifying the difference between belief and thought. The belief/state relationship is often where the dysfunction and/or feeling of limits occur in the first place, by changing physical behavior – to include internal thought processes – a change in state and dysfunctional filters occurs.

DEMONSTRATION

For this demonstration consider two events in your life. For this exercise you will need a piece of paper and something with which to write. Once you have these items, please continue.

On your paper I would like you to write two words symbolizing the following two events. The first is one that you remember as being enjoyable. This could be something that was joyful such as a time when you received a nice surprise or other good news. The second could merely be a time when you were bored or perhaps brings mildly unpleasant emotions. This could be a time that you received less than responsive customer service. I suggest that you write the word representing the pleasant event on the left side of your paper and the word for the unpleasant event on the right.

Below each word write answers to the following:

1.   What time of day did the event occur?

2.   What was the month that the event occurred?

3.   What was the weather when the event occurred?

4.   What was one reason that you felt the way you do about the event? In other words, what value or belief led you to form your opinion the way that you did?

Next, I would like you to cross out the word that represents the positive event and then write it on top of the negative word. Cross out the negative word. Imagine that positive event happening at the time, month, and the same weather conditions, which you previously associated with the negative event. Calm your mind and body and attempt to see how your emotions have changed.

Now repeat this exercise by writing the negative word over the crossed out positive word. Try to think of the positive event occurring during the same time of day and month and with the same weather conditions that you previously associated with the positive word. Again, notice how your emotions change.

ABOUT THE AUTHOR

This series is by Tim Brunson, who holds both Doctor of Clinical Hypnotherapy and Doctor of Philosophy Clinical Hypnotherapy degrees, has practiced hypnotherapy for 29 years with clients and patients referred to him by medical and mental health practitioners, has trained clinicians internationally, and has almost 3,000 hours of training much of which was medical and mental health related. Many of his courses are already available through Amazon in either short-read or longer books.

RESOURCES

General:

The International Hypnosis Research Institute

IHRI membership

Advanced-Neuro-Noetic-Hypnosis

Courses

Books, E-Books, And Audiobooks:

Sets

Elman Hypnotherapy: Beyond the Basics

Improving Your Performance Genius

Enhancing Performance: Unleashing Your True Potential (Bundled)

Innovations in Mind/Body Therapies

The Mind/Body Connection

The New Biology

The Neurology of Mind/Body Health

Transformation Revisited

The Immune System Primer

Using Imagery to Heal

A Quick Pain Management Primer

Healing the Body Basics

The Mind, Surgery, and Recovery

Calming Your Gut

Innovations in Mind/Body Therapies (Bundled)

The Neurology of Suggestion Series

The Neurology of Suggestion

Advanced Hypnotherapy Protocols and Applications

The Neurology of Suggestion Series (Bundled)

The Neurology of Suggestion Basics

Change: A New Paradigm for Transformation

Brain Potential: Enhancing and Inhibiting for Peak Performance

Reshaping: Changing your Brain and Body

Mastering Change: 10 Principles for Transformation

Achieving Lasting Change: A System for Transformation

Neurology of Suggestion Applications

The Neurology of Suggestion Basics (Bundled)

Neuro Linguistic Programming Basics

Mastering the NLP Communication Model

Developing Instant Rapport

The Basis of NLP Techniques

Modeling Behavior

Practical NLP Applications

Neuro Linguistic Programming Basics (Bundled)

Individual Books

Advanced Hypnotherapy Script Writing Techniques

Clinical Hypnotherapy Fundamentals

Healing the Body

Healing the Mind

New Directions in Hypnotherapy

Rapid Change: The Secrets of Lasting Personal and Group Transformation

Space/Time-based Interventions: Simple techniques that enhance hypnotherapy